Broken Tambourine

/tæmbəˈrin/

鈴鼓

Nick Yapp

Illustrated by Jacqui Thomas

HODDER AND STOUGHTON

LONDON SYDNEY AUCKLAND TORONTO

British Library Cataloguing in Publication Data

Yapp, Nick
 The broken tambourine.—(Hopscotch)
 I. Title   II. Thomas, Jacqui
 823'.914[J]   PZ7

 ISBN 0–340–38805–6

First published 1987

Published by Hodder and Stoughton Children's Books,
a division of Hodder and Stoughton Ltd,
Mill Road, Dunton Green, Sevenoaks, Kent TN13 2YJ

Photoset by Rowland Phototypesetting Ltd,
Bury St Edmunds, Suffolk

Printed in Great Britain by St Edmundsbury Press Ltd,
Bury St Edmunds, Suffolk

Once upon a time there was a boy called
Paul who wanted a musical instrument.
He lived in a street called Launcelot Road.
There was nothing special about his
street. It was like hundreds of others in
the city. There was nothing special about
his house, either, except that there wasn't
a lot of room in it. If Paul's father hadn't
gone to live somewhere else, there would
have been even less room.

3

The back yard was tiny. And, to make matters worse, the Park was a long walk away at the top end of the street. They locked up the swings and the slides most of the time, and they had removed the roundabout because it wasn't safe. There were weeds in the sand pit. It wasn't a very smart Park.

Paul liked smart things. He liked smart clothes, but he didn't have any. What he did have were two brothers, Henderson

and Victor. They were bigger than Paul
and reckoned themselves smart. Paul
thought they were merely flash. He had a
younger sister, Debbie, who wasn't flash.
She was simply a nuisance.

Paul was good at some things, but no
good at others. He was no good at
making his bed, especially the bit along
the wall, but he could climb up the
drainpipe at the back of the house quicker
than anyone he knew.

He quite liked school, bits of it, though
they expected too much, and it always
rained at playtimes.

Most of all, Paul liked music.

He sang when he got up. He sang as he slid down the bannisters to breakfast. He sang in the bath. He sang all over the house, even when his mother or Henderson or Debbie told him to shut up. He sang as he walked. He sang on buses, his mouth so close to the window that his breath clouded the glass.

He whistled. He whistled till the dogs howled. He whistled till old people put their hands to their ears and begged him to stop. He whistled till he was sent out of the classroom.

He drummed. He picked up sticks and drummed his way along walls and fences. Thursday was the best day for

drumming. The dustmen came on
Thursday, and everyone in Launcelot
Road put their dustbins out, ready for
their rubbish to be collected. Dustbin lids
were wonderful for drumming on.
Especially once the bins had been
emptied. An empty dustbin made a
wonderful booming noise.

Paul wanted a drum kit. That was what he wanted most of all. If he couldn't have a drum kit, he'd settle for a trumpet or a saxophone. And, if he couldn't have either of those, he'd have an electric guitar. He didn't dare to think of a synthesizer. That would be too much! With a synthesizer you could make all the sounds of all the instruments. But he knew he'd never, never, never be able to afford a synthesizer.

He told his mother he wanted a musical instrument.

'And after a week you'd never play it,' she told him. 'It would be just the same as Henderson and that camera. He never uses it now.'

'That's Henderson,' said Paul.

'You'll have to save up yourself, if you want to buy something,' were his mother's last words on the subject, as she took the bag of washing down to the launderette.

Save up?

Paul tried. Desperately.

He began by offering to help Henderson with his paper round.

'You can do Saturdays and Sundays,' said Henderson, who had long been fancying a lie-in at the weekend.

'Sure. Right. Fine,' said Paul. 'How much do I get?'

'Twenty pence,' said Henderson.

'For each paper?' said Paul, excitedly.

Henderson laughed. 'You've got to be joking, man. Twenty pence is what you get for each *round*. Twenty pence a day!'

Paul stopped feeling excited, but was determined to give it a try.

The following Saturday, eyes all gummy, stomach all empty, body still half-asleep, he staggered round the streets, shoving newspapers into letter boxes.

Letter boxes! Huh!

They were either too high, or too low,
or had a spring on them that all but took
your hand off. Or there lurked behind
them savage dogs that terrified the life out
of you. Delivering papers was like
hacking your way through an unfriendly
jungle.

Still, it didn't take all that long. A paper
here. A paper there. He was finished in
fifty minutes. He went home, collected
his twenty pence from Henderson and
settled down to watch television.

Half an hour later, the furious newsagent arrived on the doorstep. What was going on? What was the big idea? Complaints from almost every customer! Sun where it should have been Mirror. Mail where it should have been Star.

Henderson tried to blame Paul. The newsagent said Paul was far too young to deliver newspapers. So in the end they both agreed it was Paul's fault.

Paul was dragged out by Henderson. He had to collect all the papers he'd already delivered, and then redistribute them to the *correct* addresses.

He didn't know!

You couldn't blame him!

Yes, all right, all right. Henderson could have his twenty pence back.

Yes! And his paper round.

Never wanted it in the first place, thought Paul.

His school had recently held a Bring-and-Buy Sale. It seemed to Paul a good way of raising money. All you needed was a pile of rubbish. Old clothes, old toys, old books, and garden plants.

Well, rubbish was easy to come by.
Every Thursday the dustbins of Launcelot
Road were full of rubbish. All you had to
do was beat the dustmen to it.

Easy.

The following Thursday, Paul
borrowed his mother's shopping trolley,
and spent an interesting, and rather
mucky hour, investigating the refuse of
his street.

It wasn't very encouraging.

No books. No toys. One old cardigan
that someone had emptied the teapot

over, and half a pair of high heeled shoes. It was a pity you couldn't get money back on empty Dog Food tins. The dustbins of Launcelot Road were full of those.

Paul was very thorough. He tried every single bin, working his way along till he reached the Park at the top of the street.

Plants!

Hundreds of them!

Well, of course, it wouldn't do to dig them out of the ground – but there was a whole heap lying on the path over there. Perhaps they were extras. Not wanted.

Best to make sure. Best to ask permission.

Paul found the Park Keeper.

He pointed to the heap of plants.

'Do you want those?' he said.

The Park Keeper shook his head.

'Can I have them?'

'Do what you like with them,' said the Park Keeper.

Paul grabbed them and shoved them in his mother's shopping trolley.

He ran home, hid the trolley in his room, and hurried to school.

After school, he raced home, arranged the plants on the low wall at the front of his house, and waited for customers.

He didn't get any, though one or two passers-by laughed.

It was Victor who finally pointed out, just as it was getting dark, that the plants were weeds. And it was Debbie who told mother that Paul was responsible for the mud and old leaves at the bottom of the shopping trolley.

For a moment, Paul felt like giving up. But he *had* to have a musical instrument. He had to get some money.

Washing cars! That was the thing! He

knew other boys who made good money washing cars. Fifty pence a car. Some experts talked of as much as a pound from really satisfied customers.

And this time, he'd make no mistake. He'd do it all properly. He even asked his mother if he could borrow the plastic bucket she kept under the sink in the kitchen.

Feeling quite important, as well as excited, Paul set off with bucket, sponge and rags. He found a customer a few doors down the street – a man with a beard – who patted Paul on the head, and said he liked to see kids with a bit of 'enterprise'. Paul had no idea what the man with the beard meant, but he filled his bucket with warm, sudsy water, and set to work.

It took a long time, but soon the car
was covered with lather.

'Great,' said the man with the beard.
'Tell you what, kiddo. I'll fix up the hose.
That'll make rinsing all those bubbles
away a lot easier. Then you can dry it off
and give it a wax polish.'

There hadn't been any mention of wax polish before. It did seem a lot of work for fifty pence, but Paul was determined to succeed.

The man with the beard gave him the hose, turned on the tap and went back into the house.

Hosing was fun. Paul had to admit that. What a great way to earn fifty pence! The water bounced off the roof and poured down the sides of the car. It hissed on the hub caps, and roared on the bodywork.

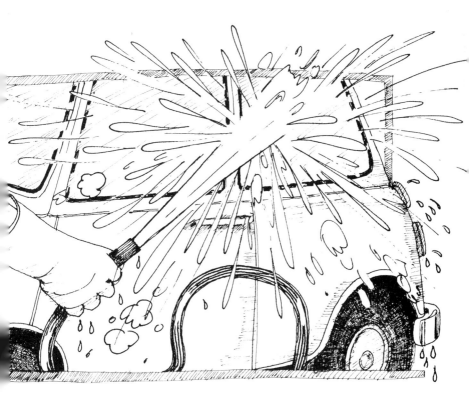

It also flooded the inside of the car, as Paul had failed to shut the driver's window. When the man with the beard came to check how Paul was doing, he found his car soaked and shining, inside and out.

Paul didn't get fifty pence. He nearly didn't get his bucket and sponge back. There was no mention of 'enterprise'. What Paul did get was another pat on the head. A very hard pat.

Paul had always liked their milkman. His name was Mick, and he sang as he delivered milk, eggs, bread, potatoes and fruit juice to the people who lived in Launcelot Road.

Perhaps Mick would like some help?

'Help? OK with me, my son. Always do with a bit of help. You want paying for it?'

'Please,' said Paul.

'Pound a round. But *only* on a Saturday and you're not to tell anyone. I could get into trouble at the dairy, otherwise, employing a youngster like you.'

A pound! Better than Henderson's miserable twenty pence. A pound – why, a few weeks, and he'd be able to get a trumpet.

'Right, my son,' said Mick. 'You do this side of the road, and I'll do the other. Just deliver what I tell you where I tell you.'

Mick found himself repeating those instructions many times in the next quarter of an hour.

'Just deliver *what* I tell you, *where* I tell you!'

Mick's voice got louder and louder.

'I said "*four* pints at number 2, and *two* pints at number 4". Not . . . Oh, never mind – I'll do it!'

Mick stopped singing.
Paul became anxious.
A bottle was dropped.

In the end, Mick gave Paul ten pence to go away.

There was a small parade of shops at the bottom end of Launcelot Road. One was the launderette Paul's mother used. One was the newsagent that Henderson worked for. One was the grocer's, and one was a junk shop.

Paul went to the junk shop with his ten pence. The window was bunged with musical instruments. There was a clarinet, a trumpet, several guitars, and a drum kit. There could be no harm in asking. Paul went in.

As he pushed the door open, a bell jangled. Mr Oldbury, the owner of the shop, shuffled out of the back room, coughing, and wiping his face. He didn't look happy. Or generous.

But there could be no harm in asking.

'Please, how much are the drums?' asked Paul.

Oldbury coughed again, and gave Paul an unfriendly look.

'Ninety-five pounds.'

Paul hadn't expected them to be ten pence, so he wasn't very disappointed.

'You've not got ninety-five pounds, have you,' said Oldbury, nodding his head as though he'd been very clever to guess that.

'How much is the trumpet?' said Paul.

'Forty-two pounds, with case and mute. There's a book goes with it, somewhere. And you've not got forty-two pounds, either, eh?' Oldbury gave a little snort of laughter at his own wit.

Paul hadn't held out much hope for the trumpet.

'How much is the clarinet?'

'Nineteen fifty. Not got that, eh?'

Well, there were still the guitars, and the violins, some of which ought to be cheap, because they looked very old.

'How much are the guitars?'

'The cheapest one is fifteen quid.'
Oldbury looked at Paul through narrow
eyes. Even for him the joke was
beginning to wear thin. 'The violins start
at ten,' he said. 'Just how much have you
got?'

'Ten pence,' said Paul, holding up the
coin for Oldbury to see.

'You clear out, sonny,' spluttered
Oldbury. 'Comin' in 'ere . . . .'

'Just a minute,' said Paul. He had
noticed a mouth-organ in the corner of
the window. He pointed to it, and in so
doing knocked over a tennis racquet,
three pairs of boots, two golf clubs and a
fishing rod.

Oldbury came round the counter.

Paul began to pick up the golf clubs.

'You leave them things alone,' said Oldbury.

But, underneath the boots, Paul saw what looked like a tambourine on the floor, by a pile of old gramophone records. He pulled it out. It was a tambourine. A very old one, with only one jingle left.

'How much . . .?' Paul began.

'Give me the ten pence. Take the thing! Now, get out!'

Paul clutched the tambourine and ran home.

He got home as his mother was cooking the tea.

'Look,' he said.

'Don't put things on the table. Debbie, set the places. Tea'll be ready in a minute or two. Victor and Paul, go and wash your hands.'

'But I've just bought this . . .'

'Go and wash your hands!'

Paul left the tambourine on the table and went to the sink. As he stood there, washing his hands, he heard his mother say:

'I told you not to put that on the table!'

She was very angry, and she threw the tambourine right across the room. It hit the wall, and broke.

There was a silence.

Then Paul's mother said: 'Leave those bits where they are, and come and sit at the table for tea.'

It was a quiet meal.

After tea, Paul picked up what was left of his tambourine. The wooden frame was smashed, and the jingle was broken in two. Among the pieces were what looked like seeds, but of shiny metal. They seemed to have come out of the jingle. They looked a bit like grains of rice.

Paul held one in the palm of his hand, and wondered what it was. It looked like a seed, yes. But what sort of a seed came out of a musical instrument?

He showed them to his mother.

'I'm sorry,' she said. 'I'm sorry about your tambourine.'

There was a long pause.

'Why don't you plant the seeds?'

'Where?' said Paul.

'There's an old tub in the yard. You could fill it with earth.'

Paul went out into the yard.

First of all, he tried to decide where to stand the tub. In the shade? Or in the sun? He looked at the seeds. They were shiny, like the sun, so he put it in the sunshine. He dragged it across the yard, and stood it in the one patch that ever got any sun.

Then he filled the tub with earth, carefully placing the seeds in the middle.

Then he cleaned out a milk bottle, filled it with water, and poured the water on to the earth.

Then he went indoors and watched television.

Every day, for a month, Paul watered the earth. Every day he weeded the tub. And every day, he sang to it.

His brothers and sister mocked him.

For a month, nothing happened.

Then, Paul noticed a small metal rod, poking through the dark earth in the centre of the tub.

Each day it grew.

'Not much good watering metal,' sneered Henderson. 'You'll give it rust. Better use oil.'

Although it wasn't kindly meant, Paul took his brother's advice.

In the sixth week, other metal rods appeared on the central one, like branches on a tree.

By the eighth week, the metal tree was as tall as Paul. A fortnight later, it was as tall as Henderson, and, a month later, it was taller than his mother.

'Should fetch something for scrap,' said Debbie.

Paul wanted to hit her, but, when he saw how envious she looked, he merely threw a lump of earth at her.

When the tree came up to the window of
the back bedroom, where Paul and Victor
and Henderson slept, it stopped growing.
   'It's dead,' thought Paul.

He undressed in a bad mood that night,
flinging his clothes about the room, and
being told off by his mother. When she
left for the Social Club in the High Street,
Paul had his revenge by going to bed in
his vest and pants, spurning the pyjamas
she had put out for him.

But he was wrong. The tree wasn't dead.

Next morning, when Paul woke up,
the room seemed very dark.
Overshadowed. He went to the window
and peered out.

The tree had burst into fruit.

And what fruit!

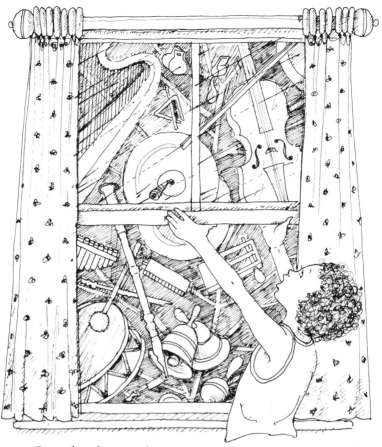

On the branches were drums, cymbals, bright shiny trumpets. There were clarinets, black as liquorice. There were flutes and oboes, and golden French horns, their bells opening like flowers to the early morning sun. And there were violins, cellos, double basses, fat and glowing. There were dark, ripe marimbas. And sousaphones, coiled like serpents round the branches.

In vest and pants, Paul rushed downstairs and into the yard.

He picked off a drum and a couple of drumsticks.

Tentatively, he tapped.

Yes, it was all right. You *could* play them.

And there was one of everything!

He gazed up through the branches at the guitars and trombones and zithers and piccolos and celestes and glockenspiels and sitars and . . . and . . .

But there *was* one instrument missing.
There was no tambourine.